FOLLOW

Dearest Bhua.
Especially for you
Lots of love
Pinky xx.

Dedicated to my mum...

Happy 70th Birthday Mum!

The Bance's

Meet us! We are the Bance's and I am Mrs B (also known as Geeta Bance), pictured here with me is Mr B and our little man Neal. I am a mum to one, wife, daughter, sister, a key-worker in Adult Social Care....the resume of what I am is a long one!

I started my food recipe blog at the peak of the COVID-19 pandemic in April 2020. Being a key-worker during this time was no fun and games. The reality of what this virus was doing was hitting home fast. With the stresses of the pandemic looming over me, cooking was the only way I found I was able to express myself during this new norm we were beginning to live. Being in the kitchen is something I have always enjoyed. I have thought on many occasions to start a recipe blog but always put it off, until that moment when I thought to myself, I'm doing it!

Thank you to all the followers I have on my Instagram and Facebook and a huge thank you to you for purchasing this book. Not only are you supporting me, you are also helping me make my dreams come true.

Please note, this book was not created by a chef, it was created by a mum who's just winging it in the kitchen!

Contents

Colour Key

Meat	Fish	Vegan	Vegetarian

Desi Chicken Curry

Serves 2-3 people

Ingredients:

- 80g butter
- 200g finely chopped onions
- 500g chicken breasts diced
- 3-5 finger chillies chopped finely - depending on how spicy you like it
- 400g tin of chopped tomatoes
- 1 tsp garam masala
- 1 tsp turmeric
- ¼ tsp chilli powder
- ¼ tsp tandoori masala
- 1 cube of frozen garlic or 1 tbsp of garlic paste
- 1 cube of frozen ginger or 1 tbsp of ginger paste
- 150ml water
- semi dried parsley and scotch bonnet chillies to garnish (optional)

Method:

1. On a medium heat, in a pan (which has a lid) melt the butter. Once the butter is melted add the onions and mix together. Put the lid on the pan and cook the onions for 4-5 minutes.

2. Add the chillies, ginger and garlic and mix together. Put the lid on the pan and cook for 3-4 minutes.

3. Add the tomato tin and mix together well. At this point lower the heat, put the lid on the pan and cook for 5-7 minutes.

4. Add the garam masala, turmeric, salt, tandoori masala and chilli powder and mix well together. Put the lid on the pan and cook for around 10 minutes, still on a low heat.

5. Add the chicken, mix well together, put the lid on and let this cook for 15 minutes on a medium heat on the hob.

6. Add the water, mix well together, put the lid back on and let the curry cook for a further 25-30 minutes on a low heat. Stir the curry every 10 minutes. The chicken curry will then be ready. Add the garnish and enjoy.

Vegtastic Vegan Sabji

Serves 4-5 people

Ingredients:

- 600g of potatoes - chopped into medium sized cubes
- 400g carrots, sweetcorn & peas. I've used a frozen mix but you can use fresh
- 220g chopped tomatoes from a tin
- 1 small onion finely chopped
- 1-2 finger chillies finely chopped (optional)
- ½ tbsp of ginger (fresh or frozen)
- ½ tbsp of garlic (fresh or frozen)
- 100ml veg oil
- 120ml water
- 2 tsp cumin seeds
- 1¼ tsp turmeric
- 1 tsp garam masala
- 1 tsp salt or to taste

Method:

1. You will need to boil the potatoes in water with half a teaspoon of salt until they are soft. Making sure that you do not cook them to a point that they are over cooked and mushy. Leave aside once done.

All the below on a medium-low heat:

2. Heat the oil. Then add the cumin seeds and cook for 1-2 minutes until the seeds become slightly brown in colour. Add the onions, stir and cook until the onions have become soft.

3. Add the ginger, garlic and chillies and cook for 3-5 minutes with regular stirs in between.

4. Add the tomatoes and water, stir the mixture and cook this for 3-4 minutes.

5. Take the mixture away from the heat and blend with either a hand blender or pour into a blending machine until completely smooth. If you are putting this into a machine, then let the mixture cool down completely first.

6. Put the mixture back into pan (if not already in there) and put this back on the heat. If you have cooled the mixture then bring this back to heat up again.

7. Once the mixture is simmering add the turmeric, garam masala and salt. Mix this really well together. Lower the heat and let this cook for 10-12 minutes. Stir in between, making sure the masala (spice mix) does not stick to the bottom of the pan.

8. Add the mix vegetables and potatoes and mix well. Be careful you do not mix this too hard otherwise the potatoes will mash.

9. Cook for 10-15 minutes or until slightly mushy on a low heat. Your sabji will then be ready.

I have served mine inside pita bread.

Masala Lamb Chops

Serves 3-4 people

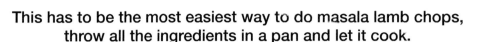

This has to be the most easiest way to do masala lamb chops,
throw all the ingredients in a pan and let it cook.

Ingredients:

- 1kg lamb chops
- 1 tsp salt
- ½ tsp chilli powder
- 1 tsp garam masala
- 1 tsp turmeric powder
- 1 tbsp ginger (if frozen 1 cube, if fresh then grated)
- 1 tbsp garlic (if frozen 1 cube, if fresh then crushed)
- water
- 25g butter
- green finger chillies – to taste

Method:

1. Put the lamb chops in a pan/pot and add water to the level the lamb chops are sitting - no more than that.

2. Put the pan/pot on the stove on a high heat. Add the garlic, ginger, garam masala, chilli powder, turmeric and salt and mix together well.

3. Put a lid on the pan/pot and let this boil for about 15 minutes.

4. Mix the chops again, put the lid back on, put the stove on a low heat and let this cook for half an hour. Remember to stir every 10-15 minutes.

5. After the half hour has passed, you could either:
- Add the butter, fresh green chillies and mix well or, simply just mix well

6. Turn the heat to high for a further 20-30 minutes or, until the remaining water has evaporated. Your lamb chops are now ready to eat! I usually serve these with naan bread and salad.

Paneer Butter Delight

Serves 3-4 people

Ingredients:

- 500g diced paneer
- oil for deep frying
- 400g tinned tomatoes
- 50g onion - finely chopped
- 1-2 finger chillies finely chopped (optional)
- ½ tsp turmeric
- 35g butter
- 1 tbsp ginger paste
- 1 tbsp garlic paste
- 1½ tsp garam masala
- 180ml single cream
- 1½ tsp chilli powder
- salt to taste
- 4 tbsp oil

Method:

1. Fry (deep or shallow) the paneer cubes until they become slightly brown. Remove the cubes from the frying pan and put them straight into a bowl of cold water. Leave aside until later.

2. On a medium heat, put the oil in a pan, add the onions and fry them for 4-5 minutes.

3. Add the chillies, ginger and garlic, mix and let this cook for a couple of minutes.

4. Add the tomatoes, cook for a few minutes and then take the pan off the heat. With an electric hand blender, blend the mixture together. This will keep the sauce smooth. If you do not have a hand blender use a mixer, but please ensure that the mixture is completely cooled down before you put it through the mixer.

5. Put the pan back on the heat and add the turmeric, chilli powder, salt and butter and mix together well. Lower the heat and leave to cook for 6-8 minutes.

6. Add the cream and cook for a further 2-3 minutes.

7. Drain the water from the paneer, add the paneer to the sauce, mix well together and leave this to cook for 3-4 minutes.

8. Lastly add the garam masala, mix this well, cook for a further 1 minute and take the pan off the heat.

I have garnished mine with semi dried parsley and chillies. You can also use coriander.

The Ultimate Vegan Chickpeas

Serves 2-3 people

Ingredients:

- 400g tinned chickpeas
- 115g onions – finely chopped
- 1 tsp ginger paste
- 1 tsp garlic paste
- 180g chopped tomatoes from a tin
- ½ tsp chilli powder
- ½ tsp of tamarind concentrate paste
- 1 tsp chana masala powder
- 1 tsp turmeric powder

Method:

1. On a medium heat, add the oil into a pan which has a lid and let the oil heat.

2. Add the onions and cook for 3-4 minutes or until the onions have become soft.

3. Add the ginger and garlic paste and mix this well together. Put the lid on the pan and let this cook for 3-4 minutes.

4. Add the tomatoes and mix well. Put the lid back onto the pan, lower the heat to just above the minimum setting on the hob and let this cook for 5-7 minutes.

5. Add the garam masala, turmeric powder, chilli powder and salt. Mix the masala's well into the tomato sauce. Put the lid back onto the pan and let this cook for 8-10 minutes.

6. Drain the chickpeas from the tin into a colander and wash them. Once washed, add the chick peas to the sauce and mix well together. Let this cook for 2-3 minutes.

7. Add the water, the tamarind paste and the chana masala powder and mix this together well. Put the lid back on the pan and let this cook for around 20 minutes. Remember to stir every 5-7 minutes!

Goes perfect with some Vegan Fried Rice in this book!

Royal Keema Mince

Serves 3-4 people

Ingredients:

- 1kg lamb mince
- 200g finely chopped onions
- 1 tbsp of garlic or 1 frozen cube
- 1 tbsp of ginger or 1 frozen cube
- 4 tbsp olive oil
- 300g or ¾ of a chopped tomato tin
- 1 heap tsp turmeric
- 1 heap tsp garam masala
- ½ tsp chilli powder
- 1 tsp or to taste salt
- 5-6 green chillies optional

VEG

300g peeled & chopped potatoes

300g garden peas

Method:

All on a medium heat

1. Put the oil in a pan and once heated, add the onions and cook until they are soft and slightly brown.

2. Add the garlic and ginger, mix well and cook for 2 minutes.

3. Add the tomatoes, mix well and cook for 3-5 minutes.

4. Add the turmeric, garam masala, chilli powder and salt. Mix well, put a lid on the pot/pan and cook for 10 minutes, stirring in between making sure the sauce does not stick to the pan.

5. Add the lamb mince and mix well. Put the lid on and let this cook for 15 minutes. Keep mixing this every few minutes to make sure the lamb stays separated and does not form lumps.

6. After the 15 minutes add the potatoes, mix well and put the lid back on the pot/pan. Cook for a further 10 minutes, again mixing in between.

7. Add the peas and mix well. Let this cook for 5 minutes, again with the lid on.

8. If you are adding chillies, do this after the 5 minutes on step 7 and cook for a further 10 minutes or until all the water is absorbed. If you are not adding the chillies, then mix and cook the mince for a further 10 minutes. Once water is absorbed, it is ready to serve.

Spinach Puree with Paneer

Serves 3-4 people

Ingredients:

- 350g baby spinach
- 500g paneer or tofu to make this vegan
- 1 tsp salt for spinach purée
- 2 cubes frozen garlic cube
- 2 cubes frozen ginger cube
- 1 heap tbsp corn flour
- 100ml water
- 1 tsp salt for spinach
- oil for frying paneer/tofu
- 200g onions finely chopped
- 3-5 finger chillies finely chopped
- 125g butter or plant based butter to make it vegan

Method:

All on a medium heat

1. Slice the paneer block into triangle pieces and slice the thickness in half.

2. Get a large bowl of cold water and keep aside. Shallow fry the paneer until the pieces become slightly brown. Remove the paneer from the oil and put it straight into the bowl of cold water. Set this aside for later.

3. In a large pan which has a lid put the spinach in, add the water and the salt for the spinach. Place the lid on top of the pan and let the spinach cook for around 20 minutes on a low-medium heat. The spinach will reduce and release some water, this is normal.

4. Once cooked, take this off the heat and blitz with a hand blender until the spinach is smooth.

5. Add the corn flour and blitz together.

6. In a separate pan add the butter and let this melt. Then add the chopped onions and let this cook until the onions become soft.

7. Add the chillies, ginger and garlic and mix well together. Let this cook for 3-4 minutes.

8. Add the spinach purée to the onion mix and mix well together. Then add the salt (to taste).

9. Drain the water from the paneer and add this to the spinach mix. Mix this together well and let this cook for a further 8-10 minutes.

Your Spinach Puree with Paneer will be ready to eat. Serve with some naan, roti or rice!

Vegan Aloo & Aubergine Sabji

Serves 3-4 people

Ingredients:

- 1 medium/large aubergine
- 2 medium/large potatoes peeled
- 1 large onion finely chopped
- 200g chopped tomato tin
- 5-6 tbsp of oil
- 1tsp turmeric powder
- ½ tsp chilli powder
- 1 tsp garam masala
- 1 tsp salt to taste
- 150ml water

Method:

1. Cut the aubergine and potatoes into wedges.

2. Put 5-6 tablespoons of oil in a pan, heat the oil and add the potatoes. Fry the potatoes until they are golden brown and then remove.

3. Add the aubergine into the same pan you have just removed the potatoes from. Cook the aubergines and remove them when they have browned.

4. Add 1 tablespoon of oil into the same pan, add the onions and let them cook until they are soft.

5. Add the chopped tomatoes, mix well and cook this on a low heat for 5-7 minutes.

6. Add the turmeric, chilli powder, garam masala, salt and mix this well together. Cook this for 10-15 minutes.

7. Add the fried potatoes, aubergines and water. Mix well and let this cook for 5-7 minutes.

Your Vegan Potato and Aubergine Sabji will be ready to serve.

Peas & Paneer

Serves 4-5 people

Ingredients:

- 500g paneer cut into cubes
- 300g frozen peas
- 400g chopped tomatoes tin
- 200g onions – finely chopped
- oil for shallow frying the paneer
- 500ml water
- 1½ tsp salt or to taste
- 1 heap tsp garam masala
- 1 heap tsp cumin seeds
- 1 heap tsp turmeric powder
- ½ tsp red chilli powder
- 1 heap tbsp minced garlic or 1½ frozen cubes
- 1 heap tbsp minced ginger or 1½ frozen cubes
- 3-5 finger chillies - finely chopped (optional)

Method:

1. Shallow fry the paneer cubes until they are slightly brown. Remove them from the oil and put them straight into a bowl of cold water. Leave this soaking aside while you make the sauce.

2. From the oil you have just fried the paneer in, take out 60ml of oil and safely dispose of the rest. Put the 60ml oil in a pan and on a medium heat, heat the oil. Once heated, add the cumin seeds and cook for 1-2 minutes.

3. Add the onions and cook until they become soft.

4. Add the ginger, garlic and chillies and cook for 3-5 minutes.

5. Add the tomatoes and cook for 5-7 minutes, remember to stir well in between.

6. Add the garam masala, turmeric, chilli powder, salt and mix well. Lower the heat on the hob and let it cook for 8-10 minutes. Remember to stir in between.

7. Drain the water from the paneer, add the paneer to the sauce, mix well together and let it cook for a further 5-7 minutes.

8. Add the peas, mix and let it cook for a further 5 minutes.

9. Add the water, mix well and cook this for 15 minutes on a high heat. After this time, lower the heat completely and let the curry cook for a further 20-25 minutes. Remember to stir in between.

Your paneer will then be ready to eat!

The Masala Lamb
Serves 3-4 people

Ingredients:

- 1kg boneless lamb
- 175g butter
- 400g onions - finely chopped
- 3-5 finger chillies finely chopped (to taste)
- 300g tin chopped tomato
- 1 tbsp crushed garlic or 1 frozen cube
- 1 tbsp crushed ginger or 1 frozen cube
- 1 heap tsp garam masala
- 1 heap tsp turmeric
- ½ tsp chilli powder
- 1 tsp salt or to taste
- 200ml water

Method:

After each of the steps below, put a lid on the pan. This will help with the ingredients cooking through thoroughly, which is key in this recipe.

1. On a medium heat on the hob melt the butter in a pan. Once the butter is melted add the onions, mix well and cook for 4-5 minutes with a lid on the pan.

2. Add the chillies, ginger and garlic, mix this well and cook for 4-5 minutes with a lid on the pan.

3. Add the tomatoes, mix this together well and cook this for 5 minutes with a lid on the pan.

4. Add the garam masala, turmeric, salt and chilli powder, mix this together well and cook for 8-10 minutes with a lid on the pan. At this point lower the heat.

5. Add the lamb, mix well, set the heat to medium/high gas mark and cook for 15 minutes with a lid on the pan.

6. Add the water, mix well and cook on a medium/high heat for a further 15 minutes with a lid on the pan.

7. Move the pan to the smallest burner on the stove and on a low heat, cook the lamb curry for 1 hour. Remember to stir every 15-20 minutes. Your masala lamb curry will then be ready to serve and enjoy.

Ruby Chicken

Serves 3-4 people

Recipe from Dishoom's cook book, made easier by Mrs B.
Vegetarian option will be to add paneer instead of chicken.

Ingredients:

- 1kg diced chicken breasts or 750g diced paneer to make this vegetarian
- 800g chopped tomatoes/2 tins – blitzed to a smooth texture
- 35g minced garlic
- 20g minced ginger
- 175ml vegetable oil
- 150ml water
- 80ml double cream
- 1 tsp ground cumin
- 1 tbsp runny honey
- 35g butter
- 1tsp garam masala
- 6 green cardamom pods
- 2 black large cardamom pods
- 2 cinnamon sticks
- 2 tsp sea salt – or to taste
- 1½ tsp deggi mirch chilli powder
- 20g granulated Sugar
- 1 tsp ground fenugreek leaves – crush to become small as possible

Method:

After each of the steps below, put a lid on your pan. This will help with the ingredients cooking through thoroughly, which is key in this recipe. If you are making this vegetarian then shallow fry the paneer cubes. Once fried put them straight into a bowl of cold water and set aside for later.

1. In a large pan, add the oil and let this heat on a medium hob setting. Once heated add all the cardamom pods (8 in total) and cinnamon sticks. Let this cook for 10-15 minutes.

2. Add the ginger and garlic and let this cook for 5-7 minutes.

3. Add the blitzed tomatoes, mix this well together, lower the heat on the hob and let this cook for 20-25 minutes. Remember to stir in between. The tomatoes will reduce by around half.

4. Add the salt, garam masala, sugar, chilli powder, ground cumin and fenugreek leaves and let this cook for a further 10-15 minutes. Remember to stir in between.

5. Add the butter and honey and let this cook for a further 10 minutes. Remember to stir in between.

6. Add the cream and cook for 5 minutes.

7. Add the chicken/paneer and water, and cook for 20-25 minutes on a low heat. Switch off the heat, garnish with some fresh coriander, and your ruby dish is ready to shine and serve.

Vegan Smegan Tadka Dhaal

Serves 3-4 people

Ingredients:

- 150g red split lentils
- 150g yellow lentils
- 220g chopped tomato tin
- 140g onions chopped finely
- ½ tsp turmeric for lentils
- ½ tsp turmeric for sauce
- ½ tsp salt for lentils
- ½ tsp salt or to taste
- ½ tsp chilli powder
- 1 tsp cumin seeds
- ½ tsp garam masala
- 500ml water to boil lentils
- 200-250ml water for curry
- 4 tbsp of oil
- 1 tsp garlic paste
- 1 tsp ginger paste
- 3-5 finger chillies finely chopped (optional)
- parsley and red chilli to garnish

Method: Lentils

On a medium heat

After each of the steps below, put a lid on your pan. This will help with the ingredients cooking through thoroughly, which is key in this recipe.

1. Put the lentils in a non-stick saucepan and add 500ml of water. Add the turmeric and salt for the lentils and boil the lentils until they are completely soft. This takes normally between 15-20 minutes. Keep checking the lentils every 5 minutes, if the water has evaporated and the lentils are not soft enough then you may need to add a bit more water throughout the process.

Method: Masala

On a medium heat

1. In a separate pan add the oil. Once this is heated add the cumin seeds and cook for 1 minute.

30

2. Add the onions, mix well and cook for 3-4 minutes until the onions are soft. Then add the chillies, mix well and cook for a further 2 minutes.

3. Add the garlic and ginger paste, mix well together and cook for 3 minutes.

4. Add the tomatoes, mix well together and cook for 5 minutes.

5. Add the turmeric, garam masala, chilli powder and salt. Mix well and lower the heat. Put a lid on the pan and let this cook for 7-8 minutes.

6. Add the cooked lentils that you prepared earlier and mix well together, coating the lentils with the masala sauce you have just made.

7. Add 200 - 250ml water and mix well. If you are finding the curry is too thick, then add another 50ml of water until you have reached your desired thickness. Cook for a further 5 minutes on a low heat.

8. Garnish with semi-dried parsley and chillies - this is optional.

Enjoy your vegan-smegan tadka dhaal which is an excellent source of protein in a bowl of goodness.

Spicy Kofta's

Serves 2-3 people

Ingredients:

Kofta's (meatballs):
- 500g mince lamb
- 1tsp salt
- ½ tsp garam masala
- ½ tsp turmeric powder
- ¼ - ½ tsp red chili powder (to taste)

Sauce:
- 125g butter
- 250g onions – finely chopped
- 3-5 finger chilies (to taste)
- 1 tbsp of fresh minced garlic or 1 cube frozen
- 1 tbsp of fresh minced ginger or 1 cube frozen
- 1 tin chopped tomatoes (400g)
- ½ tsp salt or to taste
- 1 tsp garam masala
- 1 tsp turmeric powder
- ¼ tsp red chili powder
- 200ml water

Method: Kofta's

1. Put the mince into a mixing bowl.

2. Add the salt, garam masala, turmeric, red chilli powder and mix well.

3. Make small/medium balls – around 2 cm diameter.

Set aside for later.

Method: Sauce

All the below on a medium heat and after each step, put a lid on your pan.

1. Put the butter in a pan and let this melt. Add the onions and let the onions cook until soft. Then add the chillies, ginger and garlic and mix well. Let this cook for 3-5 minutes with a lid on the pan.

2. Add the tomatoes, mix well and let this cook for 5 minutes.

3. Add the salt, garam masala, turmeric and chilli powder and mix this well together. Lower the heat on the hob to the minimum.

4. Add the kofta's, placing them carefully in a circular pattern and leaving a tiny gap between them. This will stop them from sticking to each other. Once all the kofta's are placed in the pan, put the lid on and let them cook in the simmering sauce for 5-7 minutes. The kofta's will turn a light brown colour which will show they have set into their shape.

5. Once the kofta's have gone light brown, they are ready to be stirred. Gently stir the kofta's in the sauce, put the lid on the pan and let them simmer for a further 8-10 minutes. Remember to stir in between.

6. Add the water and mix. Turn the heat back to medium and with the lid back on to the pan, let these cook for a further 15-20 minutes. Remember to stir in between.

7. Lower the heat to the minimum and let cook for a further 20-25 minutes. Remember to stir in between.

The mouth-watering kofta curry is now ready to indulge in with rice or some hot chappati's!

Fried Rice

Serves 3-4 people

Ingredients:

- 1 cup white rice
- 1 heap tsp cumin seeds
- 1 small/medium onion sliced finely
- 2 tbsp oil
- salt to taste - (I used 1 tsp in mine)
- 2 cups of water (use the same cup you measured the rice in for the right measurement of water)

Method:

1. Soak the rice in water for at least 30 minutes before cooking.

2. Heat the oil in a large pot which has a lid. Add the cumin seeds and cook the seeds for 2 minutes.

3. Add the onions, mix together and cook for 3-4 minutes until the onions become soft.

4. Drain the water from the rice, give the rice a quick wash and add this to the pot.

5. Add 2 cups of water, put the lid on the pot and on a low heat let this cook for 15-20 minutes. Keep checking the rice every 5 minutes during this time and give it a gentle stir to make sure it does not stick to the pan.

6. When the water has evaporated, take a grain of rice and check to see if it is cooked. If you feel the rice needs more time then add some more water, usually half a cup, and let the rice cook for a further few minutes.

Your rice will then be ready. This is one of those recipes where you can add ingredients to your recipe i.e. peas, sweetcorn, vegetables. If you are doing this then add your vegetables at point 5.

Enjoy your rice with any of the curries in the book.

Divine Lamb Dish

Serves 3-4 people

Ingredients:

For the steaks
- 2 lean lamb steaks
- 3 crushed garlic cloves
- 1 tsp mint sauce
- 2 tbsp olive oil for marinade
- 2 tbsp olive oil for cooking the lamb
- salt & pepper to taste

For the lamb jus
- ½ vegetable stock cube
- 200ml water
- ½ tsp mint sauce
- 1 tsp tomato ketchup
- salt & pepper to taste

Method:

1. Take the lamb steaks out of the fridge and packaging for half an hour before you marinate them.

2. In a small bowl add the olive oil, crushed garlic, salt, pepper and mint sauce. Mix this together well.

3. Cover the lamb steaks in the marinade and leave them in the sauce for 30 minutes before cooking.

4. To cook the steaks, in a pan add 2 tbsp of olive oil and let this heat. Place the lamb steaks on the heated pan and let this cook on both sides.

5. Once the steaks are cooked remove the steaks from the pan. With the same pan on the hob start making the lamb jus. Add the water to the pan and with a fish-slice or wooden spoon scrape the bottom of the pan where the lamb juices would of set.

6. Bring the water to simmer and add the stock cube. Mix this well until the stock has not dissolved.

7. Add the mint sauce and ketchup to the pan and mix well. Let this simmer for 5-7 minutes. The lamb jus will then be ready to pour on the lamb.

Aubergine Bake

Serves 3-4 people

Ingredients:

- 2 x aubergines
- 150g shallots - finely chopped
- 1 x stock pot
- breadcrumbs
- 600g chopped tomatoes tin
- 1 tbsp oregano herbs
- 1 tbsp of garlic salt
- 1 x mozzarella ball do not add if vegan
- fresh green pesto do not add if vegan

Method:

If Vegan skip to step 9 & 10

1. Slice the aubergine into thin slices.

2. Add a splash of olive oil to a frying pan, and on low-medium heat, cook the aubergine slices on both sides until they brown. You may find that the slices do not all fit on one pan, you will need to repeat the above process until all the aubergine slices are cooked. Once this is done, leave aside.

3. In the same pan, keeping the hob on a low-medium heat, add 3 tablespoons of olive oil.

4. Once this has heated add the stock pot and mix until it loosens up. Keep mixing this or it will stick to the pan.

5. Add the tomatoes and mix well. Let this cook for 2-3 minutes.

6. Add the oregano and garlic salt, mix well together and cook for a further 2 minutes.

7. Add the shallots, mix well and lower the heat. If you have a lid to the pan the you could put the lid on. Let this cook for 10-15 minutes giving it regular stirs in-between. The reason I add the shallots in at this stage is, so the shallots juices run into the sauce and the shallots do not burn. Once the sauce has cooked take it off the heat.

8. In a baking tray spread some of the sauce made, covering the base of the tray but keeping the layer of the sauce thin. Add a layer of aubergines. Add another layer of sauce on top of the aubergines and spread the sauce to cover the aubergines. Repeat this process of layering the aubergine slices and the sauce. Try to keep the sauce as the very last layer you do.

9. Create some pockets in the aubergines and sauce and make pesto pockets in the layers by dropping in a teaspoon of pesto into these pockets.

10. Chop up a mozzarella ball into small pieces and top the sauce with this.

11. Add breadcrumbs on top of the sauce and place this in the middle shelf of a pre-heated oven at 180-200 degrees. Let this bake for 15-20 minutes, keeping an eye on this after the initial 15 minutes has passed, making sure the top does not burn.

Once out of the oven, serve on top of a flat bread!

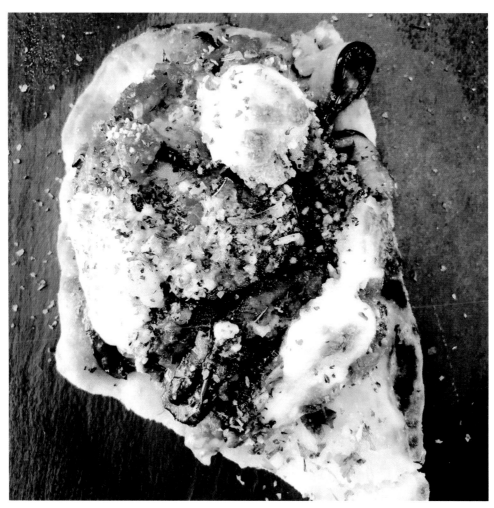

Arrabbiata Pasta

Serves 3-4 people

Ingredients:

- 3 tbsp olive oil
- 1 vegetable stock pot
- 100g finely chopped shallots
- 3 large garlic cloves crushed
- 20g chillies finely chopped
- salt and pepper to taste
- fresh basil leaves - about a handful
- 400g chopped tomatoes tin
- 1 heap tsp mixed italian herbs (dried)
- fusilli or penne pasta - to make the dish vegan, use vegan pasta

Method: Make this vegan by changing the pasta!

1. Heat the oil in a pan and add the shallots. Cook the shallots until they are soft.

2. Add the chillies, mix well together and cook for 2 minutes.

3. Add the garlic, mix well and cook for 3-4 minutes.

4. Add the chopped tomatoes, mix well together and cook this for 5 minutes.

5. Add the herbs to the sauce, mix well together and cook for a further 3-4 minutes.

6. Place the stock pot in the middle of the sauce and let it melt into the sauce. Cook for 5-7 minutes on a low/medium heat.

Remember to stir in between once the stock pot has melted.

7. Once the sauce is made, switch off the heat and add the basil leaves to the sauce and mix. The heat which is already in the sauce will cook the basil.
The sauce is now ready.

8. Boil the pasta, drain and add the cooked pasta to the sauce.

Your Arrabiata Pasta will be ready to serve up!

Twice Cooked Baby Potatoes

Ingredients:

- baby potatoes
- vegetable stock cubes
- fresh garlic
- oregano
- olive oil
- garnish (optional) with spring onions, bonnet chilli and pecorino cheese.
  Do not add the cheese if you want to keep it Vegan!

Method:

Switch your oven on to around 220 degrees.

1. In a large pot filled with water boil the potatoes until they are soft, keeping an eye on them as over boiling them could make the potatoes mushy.

2. While the potatoes are boiling, start on the marinade for them. Crush the garlic cloves or use lazy garlic. Pour olive oil into a bowl and mix the oil and garlic together.

3. Add 1 teaspoon of oregano to the bowl, mix well together and leave aside.

4. Once the potatoes are boiled, drain the water. Put the potatoes into a roasting tray and slice them in half.

5. Pour the olive oil/garlic/oregano marinade over the potatoes and use your hands to mix it all together. You may want to spread the potatoes over 2 trays to be able to mix them well separately, and then add them back together.

6. Get the vegetable stock cubes and crush and sprinkle this all over the potatoes. Mix this together well by hand. Just to give you an idea of quantity, I have used 2 cubes of stock over 1 kg of potatoes.

7. Put the potatoes in the pre-heated oven on the middle shelf. Let the potatoes bake for 25-30 minutes or until they are golden brown.

I have garnished mine with Pecorino cheese (do not do this to keep the dish Vegan), bonnet chillies and spring onions.

Rustic Creamy Tortellini

Serves 2-3 people

Ingredients:

- 1 pack spinach & ricotta tortellini
- 50g garlic butter
- 50g sundried tomatoes
- 1 vegetarian stock pot
- 100g fresh pesto
- 1 tsp ginger paste
- 1 tsp garlic paste
- 50ml water
- 200ml single cream
- 200g baby spinach

Method:

1. In a non-stick pan, melt the garlic butter and add the garlic and ginger paste. Mix well and cook this for around 2-3 minutes.

2. Add the stock pot to the above and let this melt into the butter. Once melted mix this well.

3. Add the pesto and mix well together. Let this cook for 2-3 minutes.

4. Add the cream and mix well. Lower the heat to the minimum and let this cook for 5-7 minutes.

5. Add the water and mix well together. Let this cook for a further 5 minutes.

6. Add the spinach and sun-dried tomatoes and mix well together. Let this cook on a low heat for around 8-10 minutes. After this, switch off the hob.

7. Cook the tortellini, you may want to do this without salt. The sauce is a salty sauce and I would advise to taste the sauce before adding any salt into the water of the pasta. It usually says on the pack to cook the tortellini for 3 minutes but only cook this for 2 minutes. Drain the tortellini and add it straight into the sauce. As the sauce is hot it will finish cooking the pasta without over cooking it. Mix well together and serve.

The Puff Quiche

Serves 3-4 people

Ingredients:

- 1 puff pastry roll
- 300ml double cream
- 300ml eggs whisked - this would be about 4-5 eggs depending on size
- 150g shallots finely chopped
- 100g chopped de-stemmed spinach
- finely grated mature cheese
- chilli flakes to taste
- black pepper to taste
- 1tsp garlic salt
- 150g sweetcorn

Method:

Switch your oven on to 180-200 degrees.

1. In a mixing bowl add the sweetcorn, shallots and spinach and mix this together well.

2. In a separate bowl or a jug, whisk together the eggs and double cream well. I have used an electric whisk for this.

3. To the egg and cream mixture add the garlic salt and grind some black pepper in. Whisk this all together well.

4. Pour the mixture into the mixing bowl with the spinach mix. Mix this well together.

5. Spread the puff pastry into a baking tray with high ends.

6. Roughly spoon out the spinach, shallots and sweetcorn on to the pastry, making sure the whole inside base in covered with this. Then pour the remaining mix inside the pastry. Do not fill the mixture right to the top. The mixture will rise slightly and this is to avoid an overspill in the oven.

7. Sprinkle the grated cheese on top giving it a medium coverage. Sprinkle the chilli flakes on top (chilli flakes are optional)

8. Put the quiche in the oven, in the middle shelf and let it bake for 35-45 minutes. To check to see if the quiche is ready, press down in the centre slightly with a spatula. The centre should have formed into a solid texture.

Your quiche is ready to be served. I served mine with a green leaf salad and potato salad on the side. Enjoy.

Beer Battered Cod

Serves 3-4 people

Ingredients:

- 600-700g skinless & boneless cod fillets
- 50g plain flour
- 50g corn flour
- 1 tsp baking powder
- 2 tsp turmeric
- 75ml larger
- 75ml sparkling water
- salt & pepper to taste
- oil for frying the cod (about 1 litre)

Method:

1. In a mixing bowl add the plain flour, corn flour, baking powder, turmeric & salt and pepper. Mix this all together well and then set aside 2 tablespoons of the mixture on a separate plate.

2. Add the beer and sparkling water and whisk until the mixture is smooth and has no lumps. I used an electric whisk for this.

3. Leave aside for 30 minutes. In this time you could start on the chips & peas to serve with the cod.

4. Once 30 minutes is up, put the oil into a pan, on a medium/high heat, heat the oil. You can tell once the oil is heated by dropping a drop of batter into the oil, and if it raises to the top straight away then the oil is ready for the cod.

5. Chop the cod fillets in half. This will depend on the size of the cod fillets. If they are small fillets to start with then leave as is.

6. Pat the cod dry with a kitchen towel on both sides. Apply pressure to this to absorb any extra moisture.

7. Dip the cod into the dry flour mix you set aside earlier and coat both sides with this.

8. Dip the cod into the batter, moving the cod around so it is coated generously all over in the batter.

9. From the batter put the cod straight into the frying pan and let this fry. Do not overload the pan by putting in all the cod pieces, try to do 2 at a time. This will take about 10-12 minutes. Once the cod is in the frying pan, turn the heat of the hob to medium to ensure the batter does not burn and the cod cooks. In between flip the cod over so both sides are cooked.

10. Once the cod is cooked, remove the cod from the frying pan and straight onto a drying rack lined with some kitchen towel. This will soak up the excess oil. Serve with Mushy peas (recipe in this book) and chips! I like serving mine with some potato wedges, you can find the recipe for them in this book!

Beer Battered Halloumi

Serves 3-4 people

Ingredients:

- 2 blocks of halloumi
- 75ml larger
- 50g plain flour
- 75ml sparkling water
- 50g corn flour
- oil for frying the halloumi (about 1 litre)
- 2 tsp turmeric
- salt & pepper to taste
- 1 tsp baking powder

Method:

1. In a mixing bowl add the plain flour, corn flour, baking powder, turmeric & salt and pepper. Mix this all together well and then set aside 2 tablespoons of the mixture on a separate plate.

2. Add the beer and sparkling water and whisk until the mixture is smooth and has no lumps. I used an electric whisk for this.

3. Leave this aside for 30 minutes. In this time you could start on the chips & peas.

4. Once 30 minutes is up, put the oil into a pan and on a medium/high heat, heat the oil. You can tell once it is heated by dropping a drop of batter into the oil and if it raises to the top straight away then the oil is ready for the halloumi.

5. Get the halloumi and chop 1 block into 4-6 pieces, depending on how thick you would like them.

6. Pat the halloumi dry with a kitchen towel on both sides. You may need to apply some pressure on this to absorb as much moisture from the halloumi as possible.

7. Dip the halloumi into the dry flour mix you set aside earlier and coat both sides with this.

8. Dip the halloumi into the batter, moving the halloumi around so it is coated generously all over in the batter.

9. From the batter, put the halloumi straight into the frying pan and let this fry. Do not overload your pan by putting in all the halloumi pieces, try to do 3-4 at a time. This will take about 8-10 minutes. Once the halloumi is in the frying pan, I would turn the heat to medium to ensure the batter does not burn. In between flip the halloumi over so both sides are cooked.

10. Once cooked, remove from the frying pan and straight onto a drying rack lined with some kitchen towel, this will soak up the excess oil. Serve with mushy peas (recipe in this book) and chips!

Garlic Infused Mushy Peas

Serves 3-4 people

Ingredients:

- 2 shallots chopped finely
- 2 garlic cloves crushed
- 50g butter
- 400g frozen garden peas
- salt and pepper to taste

Method:

1. Boil the peas in water for around 7-8 minutes until they become soft. Once the peas are cooked, drain and set aside.

2. Melt the butter on a medium heat in a pan.

3. Add the shallots and cook until the shallots become soft.

4. Add the garlic, mix well together and cook for around 2 minutes.

5. Add the peas and mix well together.

6. Add salt and pepper to taste. Cook this for 3-4 minutes.

7. Take the pan off the heat and with an electric hand held blender blend the peas until they are mushy. Once mushy stop blending. If you do not have an electric hand held blender, let the ingredients cool down completely and add this to a blender. Blitz this a few times until you get a mushy consistency.

8. Mix with a wooden spoon and serve with your Fish/Halloumi and chips!
Once you have tried this recipe, I promise you will never go back to mushy peas from a tin!

The Paneer Plait

Serves 3-4 people

Ingredients:

- 2 blocks of paneer (grated)
- 3 tsp cumin seeds
- 5/6 fresh green chillies finely chopped
- 1 tbsp coriander (dried/fresh)
- 1 tbsp black pepper
- 1½ tbsp garam masala
- chilli flakes (optional/to taste)
- 200g onions finely chopped
- 1 tbsp ginger paste
- 1 tbsp garlic paste
- salt to taste
- 3 tbsp oil
- 1 puff pastry roll
- 200g garden peas
- 200g tin sweetcorn
- 1 freshly squeezed lime

Method:

The below all on a medium heat

1. Add the oil to a wok style pan. Once the oil is heated, add the cumin seeds and cook for 2 minutes.

2. Add the onions to the pan and mix this together. Cook the onions until they become soft.

3. Add the green chillies, garlic and ginger paste and mix this well together. Let this cook for 3-4 minutes.

4. Add the grated paneer to the pan. Mix the paneer well with the ingredients in the pan and let this cook for 3-4 minutes.

5. To the pan add the garam masala, black pepper, salt, chilli flakes (optional), lime juice and coriander. Mix well together and let this cook for 5 minutes. Stir this in-between to make sure the paneer does not form any lumps and it does not stick to the pan.

6. Add the peas and sweetcorn to the pan. Mix this well together and cook for 5 minutes. After this time, switch the heat off and let the paneer mixture cool for around 15-20 minutes. While this is cooling, switch the oven on to 180 degrees.

7. Roll out the puff pastry sheet, leaving it on the baking paper it comes on. Place the paneer mix in the centre of the pastry leaving around the same amount of pastry on both sides to be able to criss-cross the pastry across the filling.

8. With a knife, make diagonal cuts down both sides of the sheet of pastry and criss-cross them over the filling. Brush the pastry with butter and place the plait on to a baking tray. Put the plait on the middle shelf of the preheat oven and let this cook for 15 minutes or until the pastry is golden brown. Once browned remove from the oven.

Your paneer plait will then be ready to serve! Enjoy with a side salad!

Chorizo Spag

Serves 3-4 people

Ingredients:

- 1 chorizo sausage ring – cut into thin slices
- 200g onions finely chopped
- 400g chopped tomatoes tin
- salt and pepper to taste
- spaghetti
- handful of basil
- 1½ tbsp oil

Method:

1. Put the oil in to a pan and let this heat. Add the onions to the pan and let this cook for a few minutes, until they have gone soft.

2. Add the chorizo and mix this well together. Lower the heat and let this cook until the chorizo is slightly brown. You will notice the chorizo is releasing oil, this is normal and you will drain the excess oils.

3. To drain the excess oils, pour the mixture into a sieve over a sink. Put the mixture from the sieve back into the pan and let this cook for around 2 minutes.

4. Add the tomatoes, mix well together and let this cook for 10 minutes on a low heat. Remember to stir the chorizo sauce in between.

5. Add the basil leaves, mix well and cook for a further 5 minutes.

6. Cook the spaghetti and add this to the chorizo sauce.

To garnish, I used some parmesan and basil leaves.

Crispy Veggie Tacos

Serves 4 people

Ingredients:

- 2 tbsp olive oil
- 500g quorn mince
- 1 pack stand and stuff taco kit
- 1 medium onion finely chopped
- 1 tbsp ginger paste
- 1 tbsp garlic paste
- finger chillies (optional and to taste)
- cherry tomatoes chopped
- lettuce chopped
- grated cheese
- 150ml water
- jalapenos

Method:

1. Heat the oil in a pan on a medium heat and add the onions. Cook the onions until they become soft.

2. Add the garlic, ginger and chillies (optional), mix well with the onions and cook this for 2-3 minutes.

3. Add the quorn mince to the pan and mix well together. Let this cook for 5 minutes on a low heat.

4. Add the water to the pan with the ingredients and mix well together. Then add the seasoning which comes inside the kit box. Mix this all well together and let this cook, on a low heat for 15 minutes. Once cooked switch off the heat.

5. Put the tacos in the microwave for 15-30 seconds, depending on the power of your microwave. This is to make the tacos extra crunchy.

6. In the taco shell add some lettuce to the base. Then spoon some of the quorn mixture into the taco shell. You can fill this to your desired amount.

7. Top the quorn in the taco with the jalapenos (optional), grated cheese, cherry tomatoes and the salsa which should be included in the taco kit.

The tacos will be ready to eat.

Tortilla Wrap Pizza

This is one of those recipes which you can tweak and add/remove what you like and to your taste. Goes perfect when served with the coleslaw in this book!

Ingredients:

- tortilla wraps
- tomato purée
- peppers
- mushrooms (to taste)
- green chillies (to taste)
- meat could be added to this recipe too.
- garlic salt (to taste)
- oregano herbs (to taste)
- grated mozzerella cheese
- spinach leaves
- ¼ - ½ of an onion (to taste)

Method:

1. Cut the onions and peppers into slices and add to a bowl.

2. Chop the green chillies and mushrooms (this is to taste), and add this to the bowl.

3. Take to stems off the spinach and roughly chop the leaves. Add this to the bowl. Mix the onions, peppers, chillies, mushrooms and spinach together well.
4. Add the oregano and garlic salt to taste and mix this together.

5. Cook the wraps slightly on a pan on both sides, and place them on a baking tray.

6. Spread the tomato purée, to your taste (as little or as much as you would like) over the tortilla.

7. Add the mixture (spinach, peppers, chillies and onions) and spread as evenly as you can all over the tortilla.

8. Sprinkle the mozzarella on top again as little or much as you like.

9. Place the baking tray on the middle shelf of a pre-heated (at 180 degrees) oven for approximately 10-15 minutes. Check on the pizza's after 10 minutes and then every couple of minutes until the cheese is golden brown, or darker if you like it that way. Once out the oven, enjoy them hot!

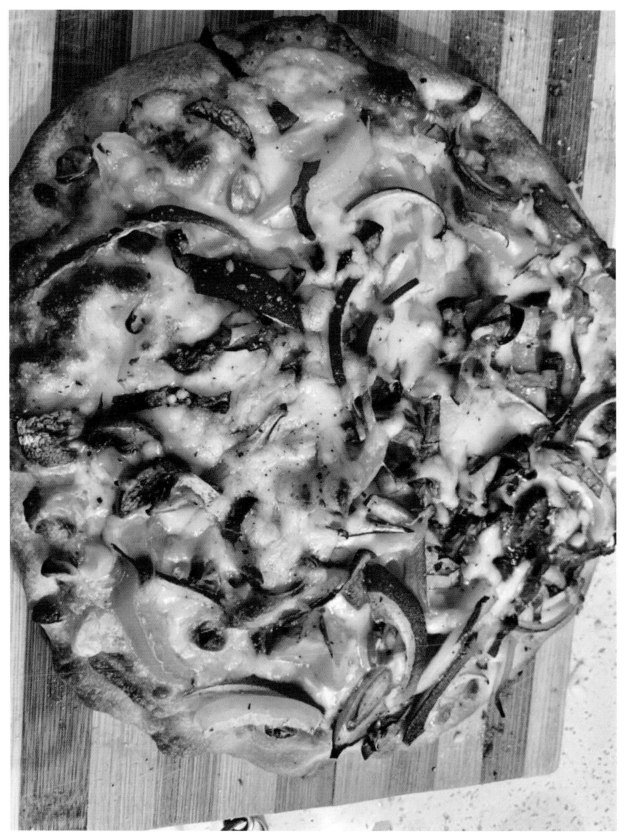

Greens with Tortellini

Serves 2-3 people

This is one of my most favourite quick meals. 10-12 minutes from start to finish! Great when I am in a rush to get dinner on.

Ingredients:

- tenderstem broccoli to taste
- 1 tsp Italian mixed herbs
- fine beans to taste
- 25g garlic butter
- salt and black pepper to taste
- 1 pack tortellini pasta (I used the spinach and ricotta filling to keep this dish vegetarian)

Method:

1. Put a pan of water to boil for the tortellini. While you are waiting for the water to boil, start on the vegetables.

2. Take off the ends of the fine beans and chop them in half.

3. Get the broccoli and cut the larger broccoli pieces to be a bit smaller. This can be done by chopping some of the stem off or the pieces with the thicker stem can be sliced in half.

4. Put the garlic butter in a pan and heat this on a medium heat. Once melted add the herbs and mix this well. Cook this for around 2 minutes.

5. Add the broccoli and fine beans and cook them for 3-4 minutes or until slightly brown.

Switch off the heat.

6. The water in the other pan should be boiled by now and ready for the tortellini. Add the tortellini to the boiling water and boil the tortellini for 3 minutes.

7. Once boiled, drain the water from the tortellini and mix it in the same pan you have cooked the broccoli and green beans in. Mix the broccoli and green beans with the tortellini, coating as much tortellini as possible in the cooked herbs. Enjoy with some crunchy garlic bread!

Chorizo & Potato Salad

Serves 2-3 people

Chorizo can be replaced with 500g of prawns.

Ingredients:

- 1 bag of Italian style salad
- 1 medium/large potato, peeled and chopped to medium sized pieces
- 1 pepper (any colour and sliced)
- Italian dressing to taste
- 1 chorizo ring – chopped every 1cm
- 2 small onions - chopped to medium sized pieces
- olive oil (some to drizzle on the potatoes and 1 tbsp for cooking the onions/ peppers)

Method:

1. Place the peeled and chopped potatoes in a baking tray and drizzle some olive oil on top. Place the baking tray in a pre-heated oven (180-200 degrees) and roast the potatoes until they are cooked and brown.

2. In a large wok style pan add 1 tablespoon of olive oil and let this heat. Once heated add the onions and cook the onions until they are soft.

3. Add the chorizo, mix this well together with the onions and cook for 3-4 minutes. The chorizo will release oils, this is normal and the excess oils will be drained later.

4. Add the peppers and mix well together. Cook this for 3-4 minutes.

5. Add the cooked potatoes and cook for a further few minutes. Once this is done, take the pan off the heat and with a large sieve/colander, pour the mix to be able to drain off the excess oils. Leave the chorizo and potato mix aside to cool down.

6. Put the salad leaves in a bowl, add the Italian dressing and mix well. Add the cooled down chorizo and potato mix and mix this with the salad leaves and toss.

This is now ready to be served up! Goes perfect with chicken.

Rustic Potato Wedges

Serves 3-4 people

Ingredients:

- 4 baking potatoes
- olive oil
- 2 vegetable stock cubes
- salt and pepper to taste
- semi dried parsley and chilli flakes to garnish

Method:

1. Wash the potatoes and wrap the wet potatoes in a kitchen towel. Place the wrapped potatoes in the microwave (all 4 together) and let them cook in the microwave for 7-10 minutes. This depends on the size of the potatoes and the power of the microwave.

2. Once they are cooked, take them out of the microwave and slice the potatoes like wedges. I sliced mine in half and then sliced the halves in 4-5 pieces. You would want the slices to be around 1-2cm thick.

3. Once sliced, place the potatoes in a baking tray. Drizzle some olive oil on them and crush the stock in your hands, so it becomes a powder and sprinkle this on top.

4. Place the baking tray on the middle shelf of a preheated oven, at 180-200 degrees, and let these bake for 15-20 minutes. Check on the wedges and if you feel they need to be more brown, or you prefer them crispier, leave the wedges in the oven for a further 5 minutes.

Your potato wedges will be ready to serve. I served mine with a garnish of semi-dried parsley and chilli flakes and serve with some sour cream or a plant based dip!

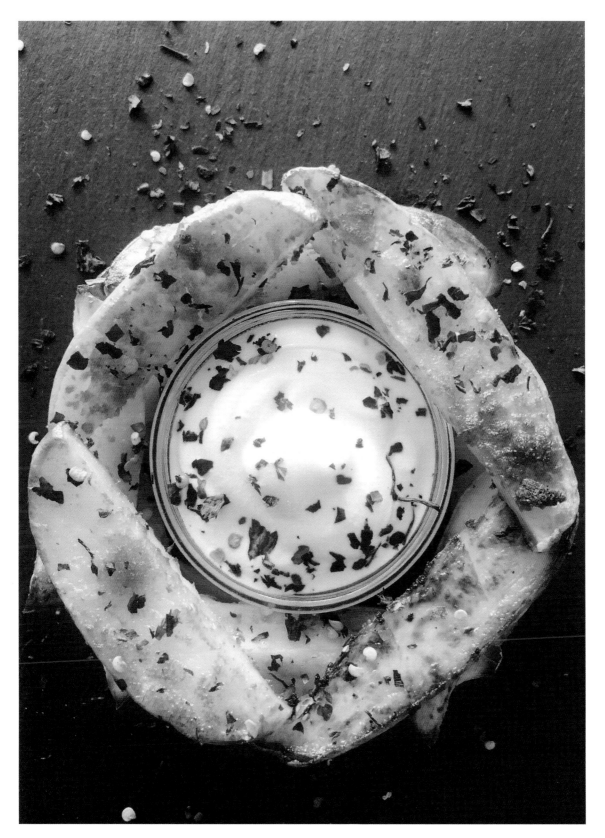

Chilli & Garlic Mogo (Cassava)

Serves 3-4 people

Ingredients:

- 500g mogo/cassava frozen cut chips
- ½ large bulb of garlic, peeled and finely chopped
- ½ large bulb of garlic coarsely grated
- 3-5 finger chillies chopped finely or to taste
- 1 tsp garlic salt
- 1 tbsp coriander
- salt to taste
- 40g butter – vegan option will be a plant based butter
- 3-4 tbsp ketchup (depending on how saucy you would like it)
- 1 tsp of worcester sauce
- water to boil the casava

Method:

1. In a large pan add the water, mogo chips, coarsely grated garlic and the garlic salt. Let the mogo boil until they become translucent. You may find the smaller and thinner pieces become translucent quicker, if so take these chips out otherwise over cooking them can make them mushy.

2. Once all the chips have become translucent, remove them from the water. Cut the larger chips into thinner slices. Once this is done keep aside.

3. In a pan heat the butter. Once the butter is melted add the garlic and chillies and cook this for 2-3 minutes.

4. Add the ketchup and Worcester sauce and cook for 2-3 minutes. Once this is done, switch off the heat.

5. In a frying pan, heat up some oil and fry the mogo chips until golden brown. When removing the chips from the oil, putting them straight into the sauce you have just made.

6. Add the coriander and toss and coat all the chips.

This is one of those dishes which need to be eaten straight away, so serve immediately!

Spinach Pakora's

Serves 3-4 people

Ingredients:

- 200g baby spinach
- 1 medium onion sliced
- 2 heap tbsp gram flour
- 1 tsp salt or to taste
- 1 tsp turmeric powder
- 1 tsp garam masala
- 1 tsp ginger
- 1 tsp garlic paste
- oil for frying
- 2 tbsp water

Method:

1. Wash the spinach, even if it says washed and ready to eat. You need the water the spinach will hold and then release to bound the mixture.

2. In a large mixing bowl add the spinach, onion, gram flour, salt, turmeric, garam masala, ginger and garlic paste and mix well together. As you are mixing this, the spinach will release water which will start bounding the mixture.

3. If there are some areas where the gram flour is still a dry powder, add 2 tbsp of water. The consistency of the batter needs to be thick and not runny.

4. Put the oil in a frying pan, enough to be able to deep fry the pakora's and let this heat. Test the heat of the oil by dropping in a small amount of the batter into the pan, if it sizzles and raises up the oil is hot enough.

5. Using a tablespoon, scoop some batter out and drop it from a low height into the oil. Do this with as many as you can fit into the pan, remembering to leave a gap in between each pakora. Let this cook on both sides until they are golden brown, this is usually between 3-5 minutes per side. Take out one pakora and check the batter is cooked in the centre before removing all the others.

Serve up straight away!

Juicy Lamb Burgers

Makes approximately 10-15 patties, depending on how big your patties are...

Ingredients:

- 1kg mince lamb
- 2 large finely chopped onions
- 4-6 finger chillies
- small handful of coriander
- 1 tsp garam masala
- 1 tsp turmeric
- 1½ tsp salt
- 1 tbsp fresh minced ginger
- 1 tbsp fresh minced garlic finely chopped
- small handful of mint leaves finely chopped

Method:

1. Put the minced lamb in a large mixing bowl, add all the ingredients (onions, chillies, coriander, mint leaves, garam masala, turmeric, salt, ginger and garlic) and mix this all together well.

2. Leave the mixture to marinate for 1-2 hours or if you can overnight.

3. Make individual patties and place them straight on to the BBQ or on to a frying pan with 1- 2 tablespoons of oil.

4. Cook on both sides. Once done, place in your favourite burger bun, add some salad, cheese and sauce.

Enjoy your lamb burger!

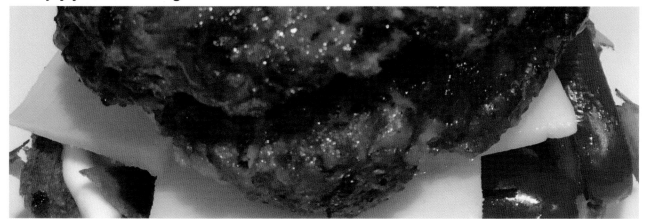

Crackling Chicken Wings

Vegetarian option - BBQ Paneer

Serves 6-8 people

Ingredients:

- 2kg skinless chicken wings or
- 750g paneer to make this vegetarian
- 1 tbsp dried coriander
- 2 tsp dried oregano
- 1½ tsp onion powder
- ½ tsp cayenne ground red pepper
- 2 tbsp paprika
- 1 tbsp salt or to taste
- 2 tsp dried thyme
- 1½ tsp garlic powder/salt
- 1 tsp black pepper

Method:

1. Mix all the herbs/spices/salt from the above ingredients into a small bowl.

2. Place the chicken wings into a large mixing bowl, add the ingredients mix to it and mix well together. You may want to use your hands for this to make sure the chicken wings are fully coated.

3. Leave the chicken wings to marinate in the fridge for at least 3 hours or overnight if you can.

4. When cooking, either place them on a BBQ and let them slow cook or in the grill and again, let them slow cook. If you are not making the paneer on the BBQ then pan fry this with a couple of spoons of olive oil.

Once cooked, remove and serve with a sauce of your choice. Enjoy!

Pesto Chicken Burger

Serves 3-4 people

Ingredients:

- 2 chicken breast sliced thin
- 3 tbsp of garlic butter
- 1 tbsp of mixed herbs
- mayonnaise
- fresh pesto
- black pepper to taste
- garlic salt to taste
- tomatoes
- rocket salad chopped roughly
- 3-4 ciabatta rolls

Method: The Chicken

1. Put the garlic butter with the herbs into a small bowl and put this in the microwave for no more than 20-30 seconds or until the butter has melted. Marinate the sliced chicken breast with the melted butter and herbs, making sure the breast is fully covered in the marinade and set aside for at least 20-30 minutes.

2. Either BBQ the chicken or you could put this on a pan and cook.

Method: The Bun

1. Add the pesto to the mayonnaise and mix well. This can be altered to your taste. I would usually do this on a 50:50 ratio.

2. Add the black pepper and garlic salt. This is optional and again to your taste. Mix this together well.

3. Slice the bun in half and spread the pesto-mayo mix on both sides.

4. Add the sliced tomatoes and the chopped rocket to the bottom layer of the bun.

5. Add the cooked chicken, put the top part of the bun back on and you will have Mrs B's Pesto Chicken Burger.

Creamy Coleslaw

Serves 15-20 people

Perfect with any BBQ or on the side with your pizza or salad. If stored correctly (air tight glass container and in the fridge), this will stay fresh for 4-5 days.

Turn this vegan by using vegan mayonnaise!

Ingredients:

- 1 small white cabbage - sliced thin
- 400g grated carrots
- 360g sliced red onions
- 600g of mayonnaise
- 1 pack of chives - chopped small
- lemon juice (from bottle is fine) to taste
- salt to taste
- black pepper to taste

Method:

1. In a large mixing bowl add the sliced cabbage, carrots, chives and onions and mix this all together well.

2. Add the mayonnaise and mix together.

3. Add the lemon juice, salt and pepper to taste. I have used 4 tablespoons of lemon juice and 1 teaspoon of salt and 1 teaspoon of black pepper in mine.

4. Mix well together. I found using my hands better to mix it together well.

5. Chill in the fridge for about an hour before serving.
This is one of the recipes where you can add other bits to your coleslaw like red beetroot, sweetcorn etc.

Tandoori Lamb Skewers

Serves 3-4 people

Ingredients:

- 1kg diced boneless lamb
- 1½ tbsp garlic paste
- 1½ tbsp ginger paste
- 2 heap tbsp greek yoghurt
- 2 heap tbsp tikka masala paste
- salt to taste
- fresh lemon

Method:

1. In a mixing bowl add the yoghurt, garlic and ginger paste, salt and tikka masala paste. Mix this all well together.

2. Put the lamb into a large mixing bowl, add the mix from step 1 and mix the ingredients with the lamb together well.

3. Feed the lamb through skewers and leave to marinate for at least 3 hours or overnight if possible (remember to keep this in the fridge).

4. BBQ the skewers on a low heat until they are cooked. You could also put the skewers on a low heat on a pan with some olive oil and cook them on a hob.

5. Once off the BBQ/hob, squeeze the lemons on top. They are now ready to be served. I served mine with a tzatziki dip.

Oreo Cupcakes

Will make 12 cupcakes

Ingredients: Cupcakes

- 200g caster/derma sugar
- 200g butter
- 200g self raising flour
- 1 tsp baking powder
- 4 medium eggs
- 1 tbsp of milk
- 1 tbsp of oil
- 1 tbsp vanilla extract
- oreos

Ingredients: Frosting

- oreos
- 250g unsalted butter
- 100g icing sugar
- 100-150g cocoa powder
- 1 tbsp vanilla extract

Method:

1. On a low heat, melt and mix together the butter and sugar in a pan. Once simmered take this off the heat. Add the vanilla extract and mix well together.

2. Put the above butter mix into a mixing bowl and add the milk, oil, baking powder and sieved self raising flour. Mix this together well. Then add the eggs and whisk it all together. If you have an electric whisk, you may find using it will help mixing the ingredients together better.

3. Get approximately 8 Oreos and take the centre cream out. The reason we are doing this is so the sponge does not become too sweet. Break the Oreos up into small pieces and mix the small pieces into the cake batter.

4. Pour the mixture into cupcake cases and put the tray with the cupcakes on middle shelf of a pre-heated oven at 180 degrees. They will take about 15-20 minutes to bake. Check on them by putting a butter knife through the centre of a cupcake, if they are cooked the knife will come out batter free. Once cooked, take them out the oven and leave on a cooling rack to cool before decorating.

Frosting:

5. Put the room temperature butter, icing sugar and vanilla in a bowl and mix together.

6. Add the cocoa powder and mix this all together well. At this point, taste the butter cream and add more cocoa powder/icing sugar if needed. Put the butter cream in a piping bag and leave this in the fridge for about 10-15 minutes. This will stop the butter cream from flopping once piped on to the cupcake.

7. Meanwhile, get 2 Oreos and take the centres out. Put them into a sandwich bag and crush them to be fine. I did this by rolling a pin over them. With the butter-cream, pipe on top of the cupcakes, sprinkle some crushed Oreos on top and add a mini Oreo in the corner. If the buttercream looks like it's very soft, put the cupcakes in the fridge for 15 minutes before eating. Enjoy!

Banana & Pecan Bake

Ingredients:

- 125g butter
- 190g self raising flour
- 150g caster sugar
- 60ml milk
- 1 tsp vanilla extract
- 70g pecan nuts chopped
- 1 medium egg beaten
- pecan nuts whole
- 2 ripe bananas
- derma sugar

Method:

Switch the oven on to 180 degrees.

1. In a saucepan on a medium heat, melt the butter and add the sugar and vanilla extract. Once melted and the butter mix begins to slightly simmer take the pan off the heat.

2. Put the melted butter mix into a mixing bowl.

3. Mash the bananas with a fork or blender and add them to the bowl.

4. Add the chopped pecan nuts to the bowl and mix well. Then add the beaten egg and mix well together.

5. Add the sieved flour and milk and mix well. At this point I have used an electric whisk to mix all the ingredients together well.

6. Pour the mixture into a well greased and lined tray bake. You can also use any other cake baking tray or cupcake cases.

7. Sprinkle the derma sugar on top. This gives the bake a crunch to it. Then place and spread out the whole pecan nuts on top.

8. Place the tray in the pre-heated oven on the middle shelf for around 20-30 minutes. Keep checking every few minutes after the 20 minutes has passed to see if it is ready. To check if it is ready, pierce a butter knife through the centre of the cake. The knife should come out clean with no batter to show it is cooked.

Once out of the oven, let the bake cool and enjoy with a cup of tea!

Indulging Pistachio Cream

Serves 6-8 people on an 8" cake

Ingredients:

- 200g caster sugar
- 200g butter at room temperature
- 150g self raising flour
- 4 medium eggs
- 1 tsp baking powder
- 1 tsp of whole milk (blue top)
- 1 tsp olive oil
- 100g pistachio nuts - chopped finely
- 1 large tub of whipping/double cream
- icing sugar to taste
- strawberries

Method:

Switch the oven on to 180 degrees.

1. Put the room temperature butter into a mixing bowl, add the sugar and mix well with an electric whisk.

2. Whisk the eggs and add this to the sugar & butter. Whisk this all together well.

3. Sieve the flour into the bowl and whisk together. Add the oil, milk and baking powder and whisk together well.

4. Add the pistachio nuts and mix together with a spoon. Do not use an electric appliance on this step.

5. Divide the mixture into 2, 8", well greased and lined baking trays and place them in the oven, on the middle shelf for 15-20 minutes. Check to see if the cake is cooked by putting a butter knife through the centre. The knife should come out clean to show the cake is cooked. Once baked, take the cakes out of the oven and baking trays and put them on wired cooking racks to cool.

Decorating:

1. Pour the cream into a mixing bowl and add the icing sugar to taste. The more sweeter you would like the cream, the more icing sugar you would add.

2. Whisk the cream until the cream becomes thick. Be careful you do not over whisk as the cream will start curdling.

3. Get the cooled cake and place the first layer in the centre of a cake stand or a plate.

4. Spread some whipped cream evenly on the top and then place the second layer of cake on top.

5. Get some straws, measure the height of the cake and cut the straw 1mm below the cakes height. Cut 4 straws to this height.

6. Pierce the straws in different places all the way through the cake. This will help the cake stay in place when cutting or moving the cake. This trick works well especially when you have a thicker filling.

7. Add a layer of cream on top.

8. Put some cream in a piping bag and pipe some swirls around the top part of the cake.

9. Add the strawberries on the pipped swirls spreading them evenly around.

10. In the centre of the cake top add some chopped pistachio nuts.
Your cake is now ready. I popped mine back in the fridge for an hour before serving, just to let it all set. Enjoy with a cup of tea or coffee.

Classic Coffee & Walnut Cake

Serves 6-8 people

Ingredients:

- 250g butter at room temperature
- 2 tbsp of coffee in 100ml water cooled
- 280g self raising flour sieved
- 250g caster sugar
- 1 tsp baking powder
- 4 medium eggs whisked
- 1 tsp vanilla extract
- 90g walnuts chopped finely
- whole and chopped walnuts for decorating
- 600ml of whipping or double cream
- icing sugar to taste

Method:

Switch the oven on to 180 degrees

1. In a mixing bowl whisk the butter and sugar together. I have used an electric whisk for this.

2. Add in the eggs and whisk together.

3. Add in the sieved flour and whisk together.

4. Add the baking powder, vanilla and coffee and whisk together well.

5. Add the walnuts and mix with a wooden spoon until the nuts are mixed in well.

6. Split the mixtures into 2 well greased baking tins and bake for 15-20 minutes or until cooked.

7. Once out the oven, take the cakes out of the baking trays and let them cool on a wire cooling rack.

Decorating:

1. Pour the cream in a mixing bowl and add the icing sugar to taste. The more sweeter you would like the cream, the more icing sugar you would add.

2. Whisk the cream until it becomes thick.

3. Get the cooled cakes and place the first layer in the centre of a cake stand or plate. Spread some whipped cream evenly on the first layer and place the second layer on top.

4. Get some straws, measure the height of the cake and cut the straws 1mm below the cakes height. Cut 4 straws this height. Pierce the straws in different places all the way through the cake. This will help the cake stay in place when cutting or moving the cake. This trick works well especially when you have a thicker filling.

5. Add a layer of cream on top and spread the cream on top and on the sides for the cake.

6. Decorate as you like with the walnuts. Put the cake into the fridge for 20-30 minutes, this helps set the cream, before serving!

The Lemon Loaf

Ingredients:

- 175g butter at room temperature
- 175g caster sugar
- 3 medium eggs
- 175g self-raising flour
- 1 tsp baking powder
- zest of 1 lemon
- juice of 2 lemons – 1 lemon for the batter, 1 for the drizzle
- icing sugar

Lemon Frosting:
- 250g unsalted butter at room temperature
- icing sugar to taste
- juice of ½ - 1 lemon to taste

Method:

Switch the oven on to 180 degrees

1. Whisk together the room temperature butter and caster sugar well.

2. Add the eggs and whisk with the butter and sugar until smooth.

3. Sieve in the self raising flour to the above and mix well.

4. Add the baking powder, lemon zest and lemon juice and whisk this well together.

5. Put the mixture into a well-greased baking loaf tin. Place this in the oven, on the middle shelf for 20-25 minutes or until cooked. To check if it is cooked, pierce a butter knife through the centre. The knife will need to come out batter-free to know it is cooked.

6. Once cooked and out of the oven, take the loaf out of the tin and place the loaf on a cooling rack to let them cool.

7. In a bowl add the icing sugar to the lemon juice and mix this well and until it makes a thick but runny syrup. Pierce holes in the sponge and pour the syrup on top. Spread the syrup as evenly as possible.

Decorating

1. Add the unsalted butter, icing sugar (to taste) and lemon juice (to taste) and whisk together well.

2. Spread or pipe the frosting onto the cooled down cake.

Pop the cake into the fridge for around an hour or 2 to let it set. Your cake will then be ready to enjoy.

Strawberries & Cream Choux Bun

This recipe was taken from @bregaskitchen on Instagram. It is the most perfect recipe if followed correctly.

Ingredients: Choux Bun

- 120g butter
- 140g sieved plain flour
- ½ pint of water
- 4-5 eggs
- pinch of salt
- pinch of sugar

Ingredients: Cream Filling

- 600ml double/whipping cream
- icing sugar
- strawberries for topping

Method:

Switch the oven on to 180 degrees

1. On a low heat setting on the hob melt the butter in a non-stick pan. Once melted add the water and let this simmer, not boil.

2. Add the sugar and salt and mix this together well.

3. While the pan is still on the heat, add the flour and mix well. Cook out the lumps of the flour by constantly stirring the mixture. Be careful as it can stick to the bottom of the pan quickly. Keep stirring until there are no lumps in the mixture.

4. Pour the mixture into a bowl and with an electric whisk, whisk out the heat. This will cool the mixture a lot quicker.

5. Once the mixture has cooled, and the whisk is still on, add the eggs one by one. I started with 4 eggs and then added another egg to get a pipe-able consistency. Make sure the mixture is not runny.

6. Pipe the mixture into swirls on to a lined baking tray. The buns will expand so leave space between each one. Put the tray on the middle shelf of the pre-heated oven and let the buns bake for 15-20 minutes. Do not open the oven door to check them for the first 15 minutes. Once baked, leave them in the oven with the oven switched off, this will help dry them slightly.

Cream Filling:

1. Add the double cream and icing sugar (to taste) in a mixing bowl and whisk together until the cream becomes thick. Remember the choux bun is not sweet so you may want to make the cream a little sweeter.

2. Once the bun is completely cooled, slice the bun horizontally and pipe on the bottom part of the bun. Depending on how creamy you would like it, you may want to pipe the hollow top too. Close the bun but do not squish it down.

3. Add a swirl of cream or some melted chocolate on top and top it with a strawberry.

Enjoy this perfect choux bun recipe!

Refreshing Watermelon Slush

Serves 2 people

Quick drink recipe to end this book, nice and refreshing especially on a hot day!

Ingredients:

- 500g frozen watermelon chunks
- ½ lemon squeezed
- 7 tbsp sparkling water
- 2 tsp caster sugar

Method:

1. Cut the watermelon chunks into smaller pieces and put them into a blender. If you can not find frozen watermelons, you could purchase a fresh watermelon, cut it into pieces and freeze them.

2. Put the sparkling water, squeezed lemon juice and sugar into a blender, with the watermelon pieces and blend. Depending on how big the watermelon pieces are, you may need to switch the blender off and stir in between with a spoon.

Serve immediately & enjoy!

Make this alcoholic by replacing the sparkling water with prosecco or vodka! Cheers!

FOLLOW ME!

mrsbcooks_official

Mrs B Cooks